Pit Pat! Tip Tap!

Written by Jillian Powell
Photographs by Steve Lumb

Collins

It is in a tap.

Nat sips it.

It is in a tin.

4

Mat dips in it.

It is in a pan.

Nat tips it.

It is in a pit.

Mat pats it.

Mat sits in it.

Mat taps it.

It is at a tip.

Nat sits in it.

sip

dip

tip

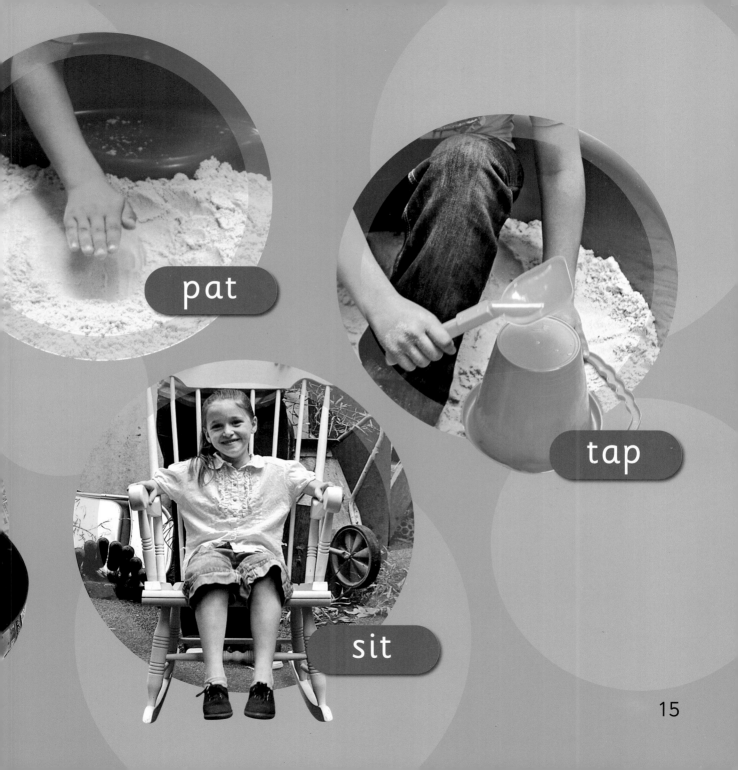

pat

tap

sit

Ideas for reading

Learning objectives: hear and say sounds in the order in which they occur; read simple words by sounding out and blending the phonemes all through the word from left to right; read some high frequency words; read a range of familiar and common words and simple sentences independently; extend their vocabulary, exploring the meaning and sounds of new words; use phonic knowledge to write simple regular words and make phonetically plausible attempts at more complex words

Curriculum links: Knowledge and Understanding of the World: Investigate objects and materials by using all of their senses as appropriate

Focus phonemes: s, a, t, p, i, n, m, d

Word count: 49

Getting started

- Write the focus phonemes on the whiteboard one by one, and ask children to call out the sounds.
- Using magnetic letters, ask children to race to make the words *pit, pat, tip, tap*, counting the phonemes.
- Hand out the books and look at the front cover together. Read the title, practising to blend the sounds.
- Ask children to describe what the boy is doing and what the words *pit pat tip tap* mean.

Reading and responding

- Ask children to read the book from the beginning to the end, taking time to look at the pictures.
- Move around the group, listening to each child read, supporting them to blend new words and praising their attempts.
- Stop children at key points. Ask them to describe to each other what is happening in the text.